HAL•LEONARD
INSTRUMENTAL PLAY-ALONG

ONLINE MEDIA INCLUDED
Audio Recordings
Printable Piano Accompaniments

PLAYBACK+
Speed • Pitch • Balance • Loop

CLASSICAL SOLOS
FOR
FLUTE

15 Easy Solos for Contest and Performance

Arranged by Philip Sparke

To access recordings and PDF accompaniments visit:
www.halleonard.com/mylibrary

Enter Code
6961-6447-3705-3721

ISBN 978-1-61780-694-0

HAL•LEONARD®

Visit Hal Leonard Online at
www.halleonard.com

Contact us:
Hal Leonard
7777 West Bluemound Road
Milwaukee, WI 53213
Email: info@halleonard.com

In Europe, contact:
Hal Leonard Europe Limited
42 Wigmore Street
Marylebone, London, W1U 2RN
Email: info@halleonardeurope.com

In Australia, contact:
Hal Leonard Australia Pty. Ltd.
4 Lentara Court
Cheltenham, Victoria, 3192 Australia
Email: info@halleonard.com.au

2

WALTZ

FLUTE

MORITZ VOGEL
Arranged by PHILIP SPARKE

00842542

CHORALE

Now praise, my soul, the Lord

JOHANN SEBASTIAN BACH
Arranged by PHILIP SPARKE

Flute

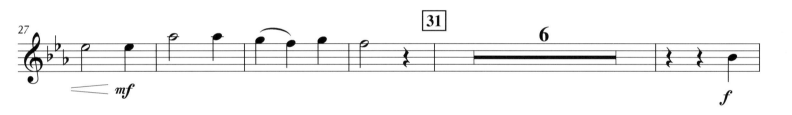

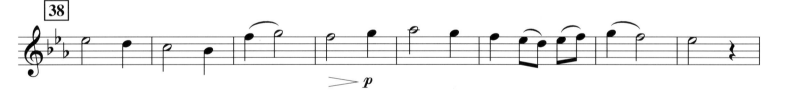

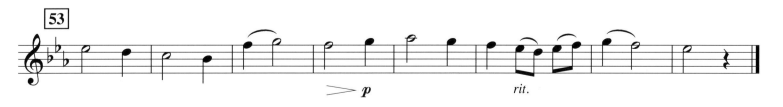

00842542

HUMMING SONG

from *Album for the Young*

FLUTE

ROBERT SCHUMANN
Arranged by PHILIP SPARKE

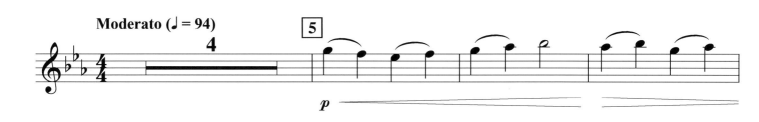

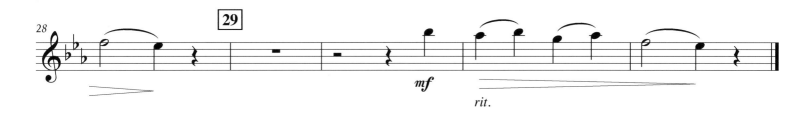

GYMNOPÉDIE NO. 1

FLUTE

ERIK SATIE
Arranged by PHILIP SPARKE

I'M CALLED LITTLE BUTTERCUP

from *HMS Pinafore*

FLUTE

SIR ARTHUR SULLIVAN
Arranged by PHILIP SPARKE

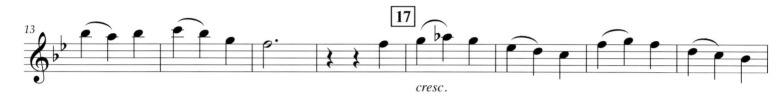

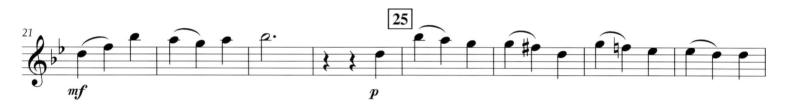

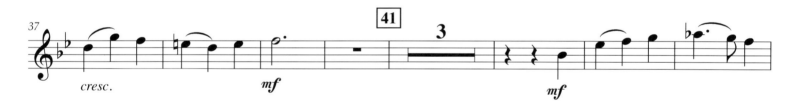

STUDY
Op. 37, No. 3

HENRY LEMOINE
Arranged by PHILIP SPARKE

Flute

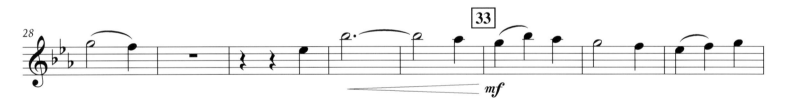

00842542

MINUET
(Z. 649)

HENRY PURCELL
Arranged by PHILIP SPARKE

FLUTE

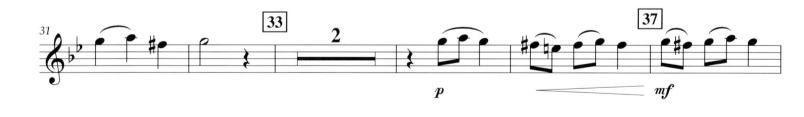

THEME AND VARIATION

from *Sonatina No. 3*

FLUTE

THOMAS ATTWOOD
Arranged by PHILIP SPARKE

00842542

NORTHERN SONG

from *Album for the Young*

FLUTE

ROBERT SCHUMANN
Arranged by PHILIP SPARKE

Moderato (♩ = 94)

TWO GERMAN DANCES

from *Twelve German Dances, D. 420*

FRANZ SCHUBERT
Arranged by PHILIP SPARKE

Flute

00842542

WATCHMAN'S SONG

from *Lyric Pieces, Op. 12*

FLUTE

EDVARD GRIEG
Arranged by PHILIP SPARKE

00842542

GAVOTTE

FLUTE

JAN LADISLAV DUSSEK
Arranged by PHILIP SPARKE

VIEN QUÀ, DORINA BELLA

FLUTE

ANTONIO BIANCHI
Transcribed by **C. M. von WEBER**
Arranged by PHILIP SPARKE

MINUET
from *Notebook for Anna Magdalena Bach*

FLUTE

Attributed to **CHRISTIAN PETZOLD**
Arranged by PHILIP SPARKE

THE PRINCE OF DENMARK'S MARCH

from *Choice Lessons for the Harpsichord or Spinet*

FLUTE

JEREMIAH CLARKE
Arranged by PHILIP SPARKE